Recipe Records

LANEA STAGG

Recipe Records

All rights reserved
Copyright © 2013 Lanea Stagg

Design and layout by Julie Reynolds.

All rights reserved. No part of this publication may be reproduced or transmitted in any form or by any means, electronic or mechanical, including photocopy, recording, or any information storage and retrieval system, without permission in writing from the publisher.
Printed in the United States
of America.

ISBN:13 978-0-615-76880-9
CKB000000: COOKING / General
First Edition
1 2 3 4 5 6 7 8 9 10

For information, please visit:
www.reciperecordscookbook.com

"If recipes were records, these would be at the top of the charts!"
- **Chris Getsla, BritBeat ~ America's Premier Tribute To The Beatles**
   www.BritBeat.com

* * * * * * * * * * * * * *

"In 1964 when I was 6 years old, I cut my teeth playing drums along to Beatle songs and Beatle cartoons, using shoe boxes for drums and pencils for drum sticks. Now you can enjoy a Magical Marshmallow Tour with these recipes."
- **Gregg Martin, professional musician and drum instructor at The Guitar Lab, Evansville, IN**

* * * * * * * * * * * * * *

"All you need is **Recipe Records** - a delicious tribute to the band that changed rock & roll forever!"
- **Rebecca Patrick, Paralegal ~ Evansville, Indiana**

* * * * * * * * * * * * * *

"Recipe Record cookbooks are an entertaining as well as useful addition to my cookbook collection. The savory recipes are impressive and fun for celebrations and pre-concert parties! The stories & song lists will broaden your music horizons. These books will add cool to your hot kitchen!"
- **Bennét Remington ~ Visionary & Beatle Chick**

* * * * * * * * * * * * * *

"If you love the Beatles, you're sure to love Recipe Records's tribute to The Beatles! I thought I knew the Beatles (and how to cook!) until I saw this book!"
- **Michelle ~ Columbia, Missouri**

* * * * * * * * * * * * * *

"**Recipe Records** is your ticket to ride in the kitchen!"
- **Michael Murphy ~ Advertising Extraordinaire**

DEDICATION

To My Dear Friend, Maggie McHugh (1967-2011)

To John, Paul, George & Ringo

FOREWORD

1964...As a boy growing up in Canada, my days were filled with dreams of one day playing hockey for my beloved Toronto Maple Leafs, watching Bonanza on our black & white television set and just being a kid.

1964, February 9th...I had just turned 9 on the 2nd. We burrow in for another cold and snowy winter. I shared a bedroom with my younger brother; a bedroom with the invisible line between his side and mine. This is where we would laugh, sometimes fight and dream of doing great, adventurous things.

1964, February 9th, 8 pm...Every household in North America is tuned into "The Ed Sullivan Show," to watch four young mop-haired boys from some place called Liverpool, England! All I knew about England was that it was a far off land of Kings, Queens and Knights of the Round Table. It might as well have been Mars! The world was a very large place back then, but became one happy family when the cute one started to sing, "Close your eyes and I'll kiss you..."

I, as did countless millions, went on a magical mystery tour over the next several years. From bubble gum trading cards, 45 rpms and mini skirts... through, psychedelia and Eastern trans-meditation, long hair and even longer hair!

All the while, the world around us, revolved at a breath-taking pace...the civil rights movement, the Vietnam conflict, make love not war, Woodstock and man walking on the moon! At each turn it was those four young lads from Liverpool providing the universal soundtrack.

The importance of The Beatles: musically, socially and politically has been, and will continue to be, analyzed and documented. However, it was the pure joy of that unforgettable evening during the winter of 1964 that I always return to.

It is the same joy that you will find in every recipe of this Fab new cookbook. Created as only this could have been created...with Love, Love, Love.

I fondly recall conversations of John, Paul, George & Ringo, around our family dinner table, and that continues to this day. The Beatles and food go hand in hand. As one who loves his food, I always recognized the appetite that the Beatles had for things sweet and yummy. From Cool Cherry Cream and Nice Apple Tarts, Coffee Dessert and Coconut Fudge, Fish and Finger Pies to Marshmallows and Marmalade...and of course a nice "cuppa." I was always curious what the King Of Marigold was cooking in the kitchen while making breakfast for the Queen.

Enjoy this book ... Eat, Drink, Love & Laugh. That's what the lads would have wanted!

Thank you, Lanea, for sharing your love of both cooking and the Beatles with us.

Canada's Andy Forgie
a.k.a Mr. Kite ~ Lead Vocalist For
All You Need Is Love: A Celebration of The Beatles
www.andyforgie.com

Andy Forgie on drums, circa 1964
Andy's brother, Moptop Gordie Forgie, with guitar
Belleville, Ontario, Canada

PREFACE

Recipe Records - A Culinary Tribute combines food with the music of perhaps the greatest band of all time: The Beatles. While I am not an expert on The Beatles, nor do I claim to be, I do have strong opinions about how I view their music and therefore, these food accompaniments. This project is merely a creative way to express my affection for The Beatles and to encourage fair-weather fans to give the boys a deeper listen, because they created innovative trends that are used by musicians today. You'll find a tasty mix of recipes, some are family recipes and some were contributed by dear friends who were excited to be a part of the Fab Food Fun. I'll never forget the special times I shared with my late friend, Maggie McHugh, and she was a true Beatle fan. She would've been in love with this edition. I enjoy sharing interesting stories & trivia and I think you'll enjoy this tribute to the Fab 4.

They were the sweetest thing to happen during the '60s and I think they continue to sweeten, soften, strengthen and lead music today. No other band has impacted music as much as The Beatles, nor left such an impressive legacy. Together, this foursome created music that is recognizable worldwide and has been covered in many genres and styles of music.

John Lennon, Paul McCartney, George Harrison and Ringo Starr were The Beatles.

ACKNOWLEDGEMENT

My family has continued to be instrumental in the success of my writing endeavors and I am grateful for their support. Special thanks to Mom, Dad, Becky and Mike. I was fortunate once again, to have ninja proofreading skills a lá Dad and Becky. To Elliott, Ethan & Abby, my children whom I adore, along with my husband Mike and Amanda, Matthew, Andrew, Katie and Jacob; all of our children have helped in some way during book events and deliveries & it hasn't been forgotten! My gratitude also my other family, Flo, Jerry, Annie and Mac. My deepest gratitude to each of my friends who added recipes to the book or second opinions on various ideas. Special thanks to my rockin' designer, Julie Reynolds.

This book is yet another example of how food and music brings people together.

~ Lanea Stagg

February ~ 2013

TABLE OF CONTENTS

Dedication	vi
Foreword	vii
Preface	ix
Acknowledgement	x

THE OPENING ACT (APPETIZERS)

Let It Brie	2
Little Piggies in a Blanket	4
Ethan's Mean Mr. Mustard Sauce	5
I've Got Blistas On My Fingers Hot Wings	6
Hamburg Kraut Balls	8

BACKSTAGE PASSES (SALADS & SIDES)

Glass Vidalia Onion	12
Strawberry Fields Salad	14
Honey Don't Salad Dressing	15
You Say Goodbye I Say Jell-O®	16
Say The Curd.....	18
Kale! Kale! Rock & Roll	20
Ob-La-Di Ob-La-Slaw	22

ROADIES (BREADS)

She Said ... Banana Bread	26
Everybody's Got Something To Hide Except For Me & My Monkey Bread	28
Tangerine Tree & Marmalade Sky Bread	30

HEADLINERS (ENTREES)

Sexy Sadie Soup	34
Scouse	36
Lady Medallions	38
And Your Birds Can Sing	40
Mundo Paparazzi Ziti	42
Stuffed Sgt. Peppers	44
Roll Up ... For the Magical Mystery Wrap	46
All You Need Is Hummus	47

THE MOSH PIT (BEVERAGES)

Pink Punch	50
Star Club Fruit Smoothies	52
Get Back Joe Spiced Coffee	54
George Martinis	56

DRUM SOLOS (MISCELLANEOUS)

I Should Have Known Butter	60
I Relish Her Majesty	62
Love, Love Me Two	64

THE AFTER PARTY (BREAKFAST)

I Am The Eggs, Man!	68
Here, There & Every Sausage Square	70
Helter Skelter Skillet	72

ENCORES (DESSERTS)

Savoy Truffles	76
The John – A Lemon Tart	78
The Paul – A Sweet Cherry Cream	79
The George – A Smooth, Mellow Coffee	80
The Ringo – A Raspberry Nut	81
Coffee Dessert Pie Yes You Know It's Good News!	82
Apple Scruff Cake	84
Strawberry Pie Forever!	86
Why Don't We Brew It In The Road?	88
I Want To Tell You About This Fab-4-U-Lous Flour-Less Chocolate Cake	90
It's Your Birthday Cakes	92
Re-Act Naturally	94
The White Album Fondue	96
For The Benefit Of Mr. Kite There Will Be Dessert Tonite With Circus Animals	98
Phase One In Which Doris Gets Her Oat Cookies	100
Tickets To Ride	102

MOVIES (REFRESHMENTS)

Well....I'll Hope You'll Come & See Me In The Movies.....	107
Penny Lane Popcorn Balls	109
Root Beer Submarine Floats	109

THE END

And In The End...	116
Cold Turkey Salad	118
Vegan Wings	121
My Sweet Pakoras (aka Pakodas)	122
It Don't Come Cheezy Potatoes	125

LET IT BRIE
(Let It Be – From the album Let It Be)

6-8 oz. wheel of Brie cheese
¼ c. light brown sugar
¼ c. lightly toasted pecans, chopped
¼ c. dried cranberries
3-4 tsp. butter or margarine, sliced
sliced apples or crackers

Preheat oven to 350°. Line a baking dish with aluminum foil, sprayed with non-stick spray. Remove crust from the top of Brie wheel, leaving the crusts on the sides. Mix brown sugar, pecans and cranberries and place on top Brie. Place pats of butter on top of mixture and bake 20-30 minutes, or until mixture is melted completely.

Serve with sliced apples or crackers.

Thanks to hockey mom, Dawn, for this luscious appetizer recipe!

Let It Be was released in May, 1970, as the 12th and final studio album released by The Beatles. However, Let It Be was recorded prior to Abbey Road, which was recorded and released in 1969.

The concept of the album was to get the band back to basics, returning to their original rock roots, minus the progressive musical influences they had created successfully. Paul wished for the band to perform live again and was hoping to ignite the magic they had when they were performing live back in their mania days.

The song styles on the album are diverse and varied, in continuing their established Beatle style, and several tracks resonate with excitement from their youthful days. A movie documenting the Let It Be project was released and The Beatles won an Academy Award for Best Original Song Score in 1970 for the film's songs.

Let It Be Song List:

Two of Us

Dig a Pony

Across the Universe

I Me Mine

Dig It

Let It Be

Maggie Mae

I've Got A Feeling

One After 909

The Long And Winding Road

For You Blue

Get Back

Little Piggies in a Blanket
(Piggies — From the album The Beatles [White Album])

2 c. baking mix

½ c. evaporated milk

¼ c. prepared mustard

½ c. chopped onion

10 hot dogs

Preheat oven to 450°F.

Combine baking mix, milk, and mustard. Stir with fork until soft dough forms. Add onion; mix until blended. On a lightly floured board, knead dough; separate into ten parts and roll into balls. Using palm of hand, flatten dough to about ¼" thickness. Wrap hot dogs in dough. Roll dogs on board until dough seams are sealed. Place on cookie sheet and bake for 15 minutes.

Ethan's Mean Mr. Mustard Sauce
(Mean Mr. Mustard – From the album Abbey Road)

4 tbsp. honey mustard

1 tsp. horseradish

In a small bowl, mix together to combine and use for dipping.

Thank you to my son, Ethan, for the recipe creation!

Graphic by Ethan Ritterling
(Circa 2003, 8 years old)

I've Got Blistas On My Fingers Hot Wings
(Helter Skelter – From the album The Beatles [White Album])

1 qt. vegetable oil for deep frying

24 chicken wings, cut in half at the joint

4 tbsp. butter

1 tbsp. distilled white vinegar

1 tsp. cider vinegar

5 tbsp. Frank's® hot sauce

¼ tsp. salt

¼ tsp. black pepper

¼ - ½ tsp. cayenne pepper

Heat the oil in a large skillet or deep fryer to 375°. Deep fry chicken wings in oil until done, about 10 minutes. Remove chicken from skillet or deep fryer and drain on paper towels. Melt the butter in large skillet, then stir in remaining ingredients. Add cooked chicken to sauce and stir over low heat to coat. The longer the wings simmer in the sauce, the hotter they will be. *Thanks Keef!*

Hamburg Kraut Balls

1 lb. sage pork sausage

¼ c. finely chopped onion

14 oz. pkg. fresh sauerkraut, well drained and finely chopped

½ tsp. dijon mustard

¼ tsp. garlic salt

⅛ tsp. ground black pepper

2 tbsp. Italian seasoned dry bread crumbs

4 oz. cream cheese, softened

2 tbsp. dried parsley flakes

¼ c. all-purpose flour

1 egg, beaten

¼ c. milk

¾ c. Italian seasoned dry bread crumbs

6 c. vegetable oil for deep frying

horseradish mustard

In a large skillet over medium heat, fry pork sausage and onion until sausage is evenly brown and onion is soft, about 10 minutes. Drain and allow to cool slightly. Crumble sausage mixture into a large bowl and add drained sauerkraut, mustard, garlic salt, pepper and 2 tbsp. bread crumbs. Combine cream cheese and parsley, and mix into sauerkraut mixture. Refrigerate for 1 hour. Heat oil in deep-fryer to 375°. Shape sauerkraut mixture into ¾" balls. Coat balls with flour. In a small bowl, whisk together egg and milk. Dip floured balls in egg mixture and then roll in remaining bread crumbs. Deep fry in batches for 2-3 minutes or until golden brown. Drain on paper towels and serve hot. Serve with side of horseradish mustard for dipping.

Thanks to my sister-in-law, Julie, for this recipe which is a crowd pleaser!

Hamburg, West Germany, was a rowdy temporary home for John Lennon, Paul McCartney, George Harrison, Pete Best and Stuart Sutcliffe, who were perfecting their musical talents as The Beatles. Off and on from 1960 to 1962, the band played seven days a week, for very little wage in the seediest area of Hamburg. They accumulated many colorful experiences along the way, and met photographer and artist, Astrid Kirchherr and her friends Klaus Voormann, and Jurgen Vollmer. They continued as friends for quite some time, Astrid photographing the band, along with lending some assistance with their famous moptop haircuts. Kirchherr fell in love with John's close friend, Stu Sutcliffe, who played bass in the band at the urgence of John. Toward the end of their stay in Hamburg, Stu died unexpectedly which shook up the band and Astrid as well. The band later returned to Liverpool after their rise in popularity in Hamburg, and it was very shortly thereafter that George Martin signed The Beatles to the Parlophone Record Label, soon igniting Beatlemania.

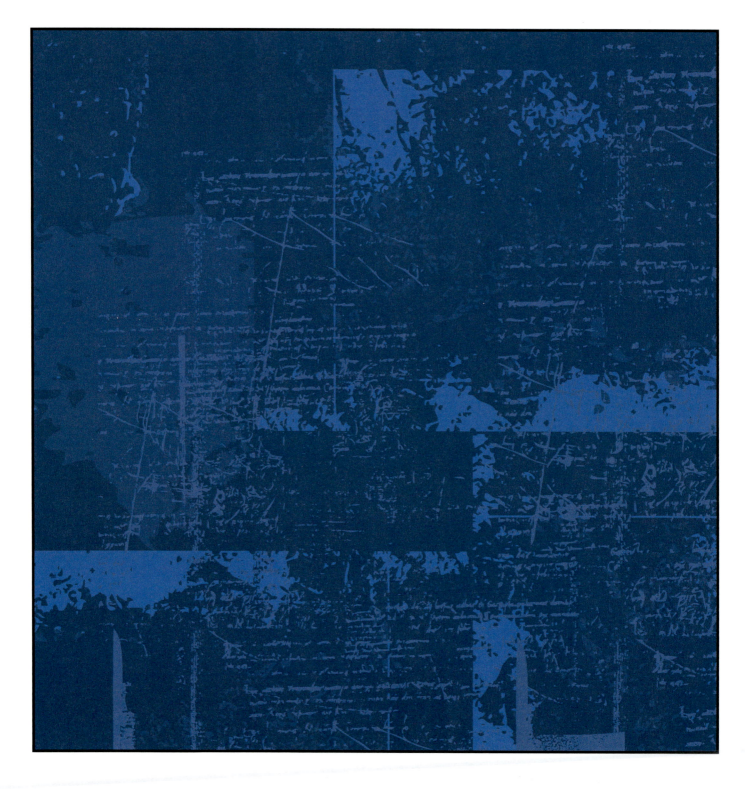

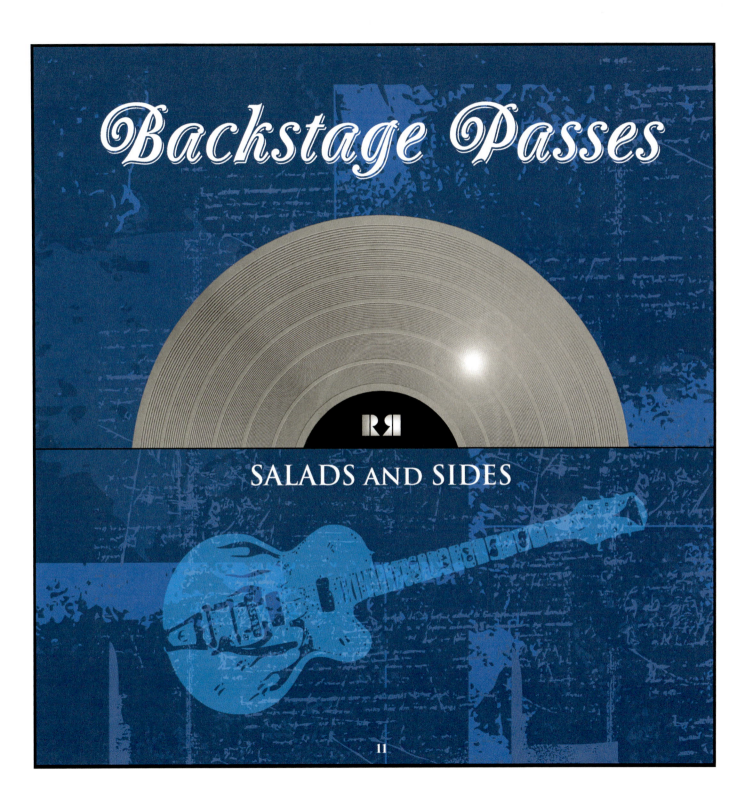

Backstage Passes

SALADS AND SIDES

Glass Vidalia Onion
(Glass Onion — From the album The Beatles [White Album])

- 2 large Vidalia or sweet onions
- 4 beef bouillon cubes
- 1 stick butter or margarine

Peel, core, quarter onion; do not cut all the way through, but leave 1" uncut. Drop one or two beef bouillon cubes in center of onion. Put a pat of butter in between each quarter. Wrap in foil, shiny side in. Grill until tender or bake in 350° oven until onion feels tender. Unwrap and serve. Can serve whole onion or just a quarter. This is similar to a French onion soup. May sprinkle a couple of tablespoons of Monterey Jack cheese on top.

Strawberry Fields Salad
(Strawberry Fields Forever — Released as a single with Penny Lane in 1967)

1 head romaine lettuce

1 c. strawberries, sliced

¼ c. slivered almonds, toasted

½ c. chicken, cooked & shredded

To toast almonds: place on cookie sheet & bake at 350° for 5-8 minutes, watching carefully not to burn. Cool completely.

In large bowl combine lettuce, strawberries, chicken and almonds. Pour on as much dressing as desired; recipe on opposite page. Toss and serve.

> Strawberry Fields Forever is one of the most complex, multi-layered songs released by The Beatles. It was written by John Lennon and released as a single rather than being included on an album, which was the practice by the record company on many occasions. John's raw, but gentle vocals create a celestial trance over the listener and has been described as his best work.

Honey Don't Salad Dressing
(Honey Don't – from the album Beatles For Sale)

1 c. mayonnaise

⅓ c. honey

2 limes, zested and juiced

1 tsp. almond extract

1 tsp. white rice vinegar

Whisk all dressing ingredients together. Cover and refrigerate. May be kept in refrigerator about one week.

> "Honey Don't" is a rockabilly classic song that was written and recorded by Carl Perkins, of whom The Beatles were huge fans. The Beatles recorded this song on the 1964 album **Beatles For Sale** and it was sung by Ringo Starr. The band performed "Honey Don't" live quite often and John always sang it, however, Ringo was pushing to vocally contribute a song on each album and he always had affection for the tune. Look for a great version of Ringo singing this song on the CD/DVD "The Concert for George."

You Say Goodbye I Say Jell-O®
(Hello, Goodbye – From the album Magical Mystery Tour)

6 oz. pkg. orange gelatin

1 c. boiling water

8 oz. carton whipping cream

2 c. orange sherbet

2 – 11 oz. cans of mandarin oranges, drained

With mixer, mix whipping cream until stiff peaks form. Chill in refrigerator. Dissolve gelatin with boiling water. Add sherbet until blended and completely mixed. Fold in whipped cream. Stir in oranges (may reserve some for garnish.) Pour into gelatin mold or serving dish. Chill at least 3 hours. May garnish with additional oranges after set.

Say The Curd......
(The Word – From the album Rubber Soul)

16 oz. container small curd cottage cheese

3 oz. pkg. orange gelatin

8 oz. container non-dairy whipped topping

2 – 11 oz. cans mandarin oranges, drained

Mix all of ingredients and chill in serving bowl.

KALE! KALE! ROCK & ROLL

½ head iceberg lettuce, torn

8 oz. baby spinach, wash and dry

8 oz. kale, wash and dry, rub, cut to size

2 c. fresh broccoli florets

1 bunch green onions, thinly sliced

1 c. green pepper, cut into pieces

1 c. diced red onion

1 c. raisins

4 whole hard boiled eggs, chopped

16 oz. bacon, cooked & chopped

8 oz. cheddar cheese, grated

1 bag (10 oz.) frozen peas, partially thawed

Dressing Ingredients:

½ c. real mayonnaise

½ c. sour cream

¼ c. Parmesan cheese

1 tbsp. sugar (more to taste)

fresh dill, chopped + additional for garnish

In a glass bowl, layer salad ingredients in order as listed.

Combine dressing ingredients in a separate bowl and mix well. Pour over the top of the peas and spread to cover, bringing dressing all the way out to the edges of the bowl. Sprinkle with fresh dill. Prior to serving, stir/toss ingredients and add salt and pepper to taste.

Although similar to a seven-layer salad, this recipe concentrates on dark green vegetables. Kale is an excellent nutritional source, but seldom used. It is less stiff if each leaf is massaged, prior to tearing to bite size. Iceberg lettuce has less nutritional value, but is lighter in color for some variation. Amount of ingredients can be changed according to size of salad needed. The above recipe is a large salad for a family event or potluck. This salad can be made in a lot of versions; Southwestern is one example. Use black beans instead of peas and add a layer of corn and a little salsa or taco seasoning in the dressing. An Italian version is also interesting, that substitutes pepperoni for the bacon, chickpeas for the peas and add red bell peppers. It has limitless possibilities.

Thanks to Betty Jo Herbert for this delightful salad recipe!

When John, Paul, George and Ringo started out as The Beatles, they concentrated on playing a large collection of cover songs, such as Chuck Berry's "Hail! Hail! Rock & Roll." The mates perfected their sounds and styles during this period of craftsmanship. They also performed cover versions of these popular songs: "Matchbox" by Carl Perkins, "Twist and Shout" by The Isley Brothers, "Roll Over Beethoven" and "Rock & Roll Music" by Chuck Berry, "You've Really Got A Hold On Me" by The Miracles, "Three Cool Cats" by The Coasters and many more.

This recipe was contributed by Del & Betty Herbert of Mt. Vernon, Illinois. Del is a member of Beatles tribute band, The Beatle Brothers, which has meticulously perfected a broad selection of Beatles songs. He also creates and performs original music of assorted genres, styles and instrumentations. He is an outstanding musician, which is a talent not recognized nearly as often as it should be. Just imagine if Paul McCartney had lived in a small town with no large audience for live music and had very few supporters....what may have happened to the history of Rock & Roll?

Moral of the Story: Support Your Local Musicians!

Ob-La-Di Ob-La-Slaw
(Ob-La-Di Ob-La-Da – From the album The Beatles [White Album])

1 packet seasoning from beef ramen noodle package

1 c. oil

½ c. red vinegar

1 tbsp. soy sauce

salt & pepper to taste

1 small pkg. cole slaw mix

Whisk together all of ingredients and pour over cole slaw mix. Allow to marinate in the refrigerator and then serve.

Thank you to my dear friend, Flo McHugh, who contributed this recipe.

Roadies

BREADS

She Said ... Banana Bread
(She Said She Said – From the album Revolver)

2½ tbsp. milk

1 tsp. vinegar

1 c. sugar

½ c. unsalted butter

2 eggs, slightly beaten

1 tsp. vanilla

1 tsp. baking soda

1 tsp. salt

1 tsp. baking powder

2 c. all-purpose flour

½ c. chopped nuts

2 bananas, mashed

Glaze:

½ c. confectioner's sugar

¼ c. unsalted butter

1 tsp. vanilla

2 tbsp. milk

½ tsp. salt

Combine milk and vinegar in bowl. Let stand 15 minutes. Cream together sugar and butter until light and fluffy, beat in eggs and vanilla; beating until smooth. Stir together milk mixture, baking soda, baking powder, and salt; beat the milk mixture into the butter mixture in batches alternately with flour until smooth. Fold in nuts and bananas. Pour into a 9" x 5" x 3" greased loaf pan. Bake 1 hour at 350°. Let cool 15 minutes in pan.

Glaze:

In food processor blend sugar, butter, vanilla and milk until smooth and creamy.

Drizzle bread with glaze, stand 10 minutes before slicing.

Thanks go my friend Janice for this delectable recipe!

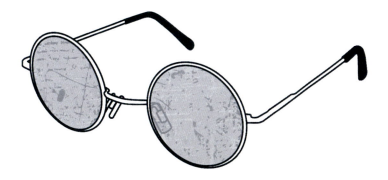

Everybody's Got Something To Hide Except For Me & My Monkey Bread

(Everybody's Got Something To Hide Except Me & My Monkey – From the album The Beatles [White Album])

- 3 cans refrigerated biscuits
- 1¾ tsp. cinnamon, divided
- 1¼ c. granulated sugar, divided
- 1 stick butter or margarine

Preheat oven to 350°. Grease a bundt pan with non-stick spray. Cut biscuits into fourths. Combine cinnamon and sugar, coat biscuits with mix and place into bundt pan. Melt butter in microwave, whisk in sugar and cinnamon until dissolved. Pour mixture over biscuits and bake 30-35 minutes. When baked through, invert bundt pan onto serving platter and serve.

Tangerine Tree & Marmalade Sky Bread
(Lucy in the Sky With Diamonds – From the album Sgt. Pepper's Lonely Hearts Club Band)

3 c. sifted all-purpose flour

1 tbsp. baking powder

1 tsp. salt

¼ tsp. baking soda

1½ c. orange marmalade

1 egg, beaten

¾ c. orange juice

¼ c. vegetable oil

1 c. chopped walnuts or pecans

Sift together flour, baking powder, salt and soda. Reserve ¼ c. of the marmalade. Combine remaining 1¼ c. marmalade, the beaten egg, orange juice, and oil; add to flour mixture, stirring just until mixture is moistened. Stir in chopped nuts. Turn batter into a greased 9" x 5" x 3" loaf pan. Bake at 350° for about 1 hour, or until a wooden pick or cake tester inserted in center comes out clean. Spread reserved marmalade over top of loaf and return to oven for a minute or two, until glazed. Cool on cake rack.

In 1968, The Beatles won a Grammy Award for the album **Sgt. Pepper's Lonely Hearts Club Band**, which is considered the biggest selling album of the 1960's. "Lucy in the Sky With Diamonds" was written by John Lennon who was inspired by his son, Julian's, drawing. The song is full of descriptive images which raised speculation that the song was a reference to the drug LSD, which John denied.

Headliners

ENTREES

Sexy Sadie Soup

(Sexy Sadie – From the album The Beatles [White Album])

- 4 large potatoes, baked
- ⅔ c. margarine
- ⅔ c. flour
- 6 c. milk
- ¾ tsp. salt
- ½ tsp. pepper
- 4 green onions, chopped
- 12 slices bacon, cooked & crumbled
- 1¼ c. shredded cheddar cheese
- 8 oz. container sour cream
- 1 heaping tbsp. chicken base

Cut baked potatoes into ½" cubes, do not remove skin. Melt margarine in heavy soup pot over low heat. Add flour, stir until smooth. Cook for 1 minute, stirring constantly. Gradually add milk. Cook over medium heat, stirring constantly, until mixture is thick and bubbly. Add potato cubes, salt, pepper, green onions, crumbled bacon, cheese and chicken base. Cook until thoroughly heated. Remove from heat and stir in sour cream. Serve with additional bacon and shredded cheddar cheese.

Beatle Song Titles Containing Proper Names:

Anna (Go to Him)	Lovely Rita
Ballad of John & Yoko	Lucille
Dear Prudence	Lucy in the Sky with Diamonds
Dizzy Miss Lizzy	Maggie Mae
Eleanor Rigby	Martha My Dear
Hey Jude	Michelle
Julia	Polythene Pam
Lady Madonna	Sexy Sadie
Long Tall Sally	What's the New Mary Jane

Carol & Clarabella are songs performed live by The Beatles, but never on an album

Scouse

People from Liverpool are known as Scousers. This is derived from a meal that was introduced by Scandinavian fishermen who docked in Liverpool back in the 19th century. One of their staple meals on board their fishing boat was Labskause. It entailed putting all the spare vegetables and meat into a pot and cooking it, like a stew.

This dish was adopted in Liverpool, especially in the working-class areas, as it could be a cheap meal for a family, when there was little money around. The mother would go to the butcher's shop and buy the cheapest cut of meat, which often had a lot of fat on it, and then take it home, dice it, throw it into a pot, and then add potatoes, which were cheap and filling, and any other spare vegetables lying around. This way, nothing was wasted. Therefore, when you "lob" it in the pot, it was "lob skause", which eventually became known, and Anglicised to just "scouse". Hence, those people who eat scouse are known as "Scousers".

Some families were so poor that they couldn't even manage the cheapest cut of meat, and so they had "blind scouse", which had all of the potatoes and other vegetables, but no meat. As you can see, we were pioneering the vegetarian lifestyle as far back as the 19th century. Forward thinking, us Scousers!

Today, around the world, every Scouser is encouraged to sit down with a bowl of scouse on International Scouse Day. It has become our trademark dish now, and can be found in some restaurants around Liverpool as part of their menu.

Nothing better on a cold winter's day!

Scouse was one of the dishes that The Beatles would have grown up with, and is still one of the most popular meals in Liverpool. By cooking this, you can become an honorary Scouser!

David Bedford
Author, "Liddypool: Birthplace of The Beatles"
www.liddypool.com

How to make Scouse for 4-6 people:

You will need:

Half a pound of stewing steak which should be diced (or use minced beef),

An onion (which should be chopped into chunks)

5 pounds of potatoes (which should be sliced into medallions)

1 pound of carrots (which should be diced into medallions)

2 Oxo cubes (or beef bouillon cubes)/ stock pot/ gravy granules for the gravy

Vegetable oil

Salt and pepper

Water

1. This is almost always beef, and can be diced, or you can have minced scouse, using minced beef. Add some vegetable oil to a frying pan; lightly fry until brown.
2. Add the beef to a saucepan, and then add in the onions on top of the meat.
3. Layer the sliced carrots on top of the meat.
4. Add a layer of sliced potatoes (about 1 pound) on top of the carrots
5. Fill the pan halfway with water
6. Add the Oxo/ gravy granules/ stock pot
7. Add salt & pepper to season
8. Heat and then simmer for two hours
9. Add the remainder of the potatoes and then simmer for a further two hours.

Serve piping hot. This is usually accompanied by sliced beetroot or pickled red cabbage, together with bread and butter.

Thanks to David Bedford for this tremendous contribution!

Lady Medallions
(Lady Madonna – Released as a single in March, 1968)

4 – 8 oz. filet mignon steaks

1 tbsp. olive oil

salt & freshly ground black pepper to taste

2 oz. Brandy

Butter Ingredients:

1 stick butter, softened

coarse salt and freshly ground black pepper to taste

1 bunch chives, left whole

Place butter into mixing bowl, season with salt and pepper and stir until blended and soft. Take a 12" piece of plastic wrap and lay it on the counter. Spoon the butter out onto the center of the plastic wrap and place the chives in the center on top of the butter. Pull the edge over the butter mixture and tightly pinch the ends, then holding the plastic wrap tightly at each end, pull the mixture towards you. This should create a tight sausage shape. Chives will be in the center surrounded by butter. Tie a knot on both of the ends of the butter roll and place into the freezer until you are ready to place it on top of your cooked filet.

Season the filets with salt & pepper. Heat a skillet over medium-high until the pan is hot and then drizzle with olive oil. Place the filets into the pan and cook to medium-rare, about 5 to 7 minutes per side. Remove the pan from the heat and pour Brandy into the skillet. Carefully tilt skillet towards the flame to flambe'. When the flames burn off, remove the filets from the pan. Remove butter from freezer and slice 4 thin "medallions" and place one on each filet. Serve steaks while hot.

Thank you to Flo McHugh for contributing this recipe!

And Your Birds Can Sing

(And Your Bird Can Sing — From the album Revolver)

3 tbsp. butter

2 tbsp. slivered almonds

2 tbsp. chopped onion

½ c. cooked wild rice

2 Cornish game hens

salt to taste

¼ c. melted butter

In skillet over medium heat, melt butter and lightly saute' almonds and chopped onion. Remove from heat & stir mixture into the wild rice; set aside.

Preheat oven to 400°. Season the hens by rubbing salt inside and outside hens. Stuff with rice. Place the hens breast side up on a rack in a baking pan. Brush with ¼ c. melted butter.

Cover the baking pan with foil and cook the hens 30 minutes. Uncover and continue cooking 1 hour or until hens are no longer pink and juices run clear.

Headliners 41

Mundo Paparazzi Ziti
(Sun King – From the album Abbey Road)

- 1 lb. ziti pasta, cooked & drained
- 1 medium onion, chopped
- 1 lb. ground beef
- 2 – 24 oz. jars spaghetti sauce
- 8 oz. Provolone cheese, sliced
- 1½ c. sour cream
- 1 c. real bacon bits
- 8 oz. mozzarella cheese, shredded
- 2-4 tbsp. grated fresh Parmesan cheese
- 2 tsp. Italian seasoning

Preheat oven to 350°. Brown onion and ground beef in large skillet over medium heat. Add spaghetti sauce and simmer 15-20 minutes.

Spray a 9" x 13" baking dish with non-stick coating. In the dish, layer half of each of these ingredients: cooked ziti pasta, Provolone cheese, sour cream, bacon bits and spaghetti sauce mixture. Then layer other half of cooked pasta, Provolone, sour cream, bacon bits and spaghetti sauce mixture.

Top with Parmesan cheese and sprinkle Italian seasoning over all. Bake for 30 minutes.

    The elegant song "Sun King," is part of the medley found on side two of the Abbey Road album. The majestic harmonies, instrumental and vocal, not to mention the peaceful sound of summer crickets, dreamily transports you to a tranquil retreat. The songs on the second side were an assortment of tunes that were considered incomplete, so instead of finishing them, they were connected and arranged as the entire second side of the album. The mix ultimately resulted in what sounded like an intentionally composed piece of musical art; once again The Beatles as innovators. This group of songs are the last recordings by The Beatles.

    The final verses of the "Sun King" melody are sung in what sound like Italian, Spanish and Portuguese words, which essentially translate into gibberish, but are twisted into a perfect bouquet of symmetry. The lyrics are strung together beautifully and sound remarkably romantic. Apparently, Paul knew a bit of Spanish from grade school and the Italian words were various offerings that the band had picked up on the road. The lyrics Mundo Paparazzi translate into World Paparazzi (paparazzi having the same English translation).

Stuffed Sgt. Peppers
(From the album Sgt. Pepper's Lonely Hearts Club Band)

4 large sweet peppers (red, yellow, orange & green)

2 c. cooked brown rice

3 small tomatoes, chopped

1 c. frozen corn, thawed

1 small sweet onion, chopped

⅓ c. canned red beans, rinsed and drained

⅓ c. canned black beans, rinsed and drained

¾ c. cubed Pepper Jack cheese

1 – 4¼ oz. can chopped ripe olives

3 cloves minced garlic

1 tsp. salt

½ tsp. pepper

½ tsp. basil

¾ c. meatless spaghetti sauce

½ c. water

4 tbsp. grated Parmesan cheese, divided

Rinse peppers and cut off the top, removing seeds; set aside. Combine rice, tomatoes, corn, onion and beans. Stir in Pepper Jack cheese cubes, olives, garlic, salt, pepper and basil. Spoon into peppers. In separate bowl mix together spaghetti sauce and water. Pour half of mixture into a large crockpot. Place stuffed peppers on top of sauce. Pour remaining sauce over peppers. Sprinkle 2 tbsp. of Parmesan cheese over top of peppers. Cook on low for 3½ to 4 hours or until peppers are tender and filling is heated thoroughly. Before serving, sprinkle remaining Parmesan cheese over top.

Roll Up ... For the Magical Mystery Wrap
(Magical Mystery Tour – From the album Magical Mystery Tour)

flavored tortilla – tomato or jalapeno

All You Need Is Hummus (recipe on opposite page)

handful of fresh spinach, chopped finely

red pepper, sliced thin

red onion, chopped finely (opt.)

handful of shredded carrots

2 tbsp. shredded Colby-Jack cheese

Spread hummus onto tortilla. Sprinkle spinach, red pepper, onion (opt.), carrots and cheese on top of hummus.

Roll up... Satisfaction Guaranteed.....

All You Need Is Hummus

(All You Need Is Love – From the album Magical Mystery Tour)

1 can garbanzo beans or chickpeas

¼ c. olive oil

1 tbsp. lemon juice

1 tsp. cumin

pita chips, opt.

Blend all ingredients in food processor. Blend until smooth and creamy. Use on Magical Mystery Wraps or serve with pita chips.

Thanks to my sister Becky for *tuning me in and turning me onto this recipe*!

Pink Punch

Hopefully you won't have any psychedelic dreams while drinking this incredible punch!

4 – 2 L. bottles diet lemon-lime soda

3 – 11.5 oz. cans cranberry juice concentrate, thawed

½ gallon raspberry sherbet

1 can whipped cream, for garnish

Combine sherbet and thawed cans of cranberry juice in large punch bowl. Pour bottles of diet soda over top.

Stir and pour into individual cups. Garnish with a dollop of whipped cream.

The 2007 film, **Across The Universe**, inspired by the music of The Beatles, takes you on a delightful journey that infuses characters from the Fab Four lyrics. Many of the songs are performed by the film's actors, but the film also includes cameo appearances by Joe Cocker and U2's Bono. Our punch recipe was inspired by what we called the "pink punch" scene in the movie, which caused the characters to have psychedelic dreams.

Star Club Fruit Smoothies

8 oz. vanilla yogurt

1 c. orange juice

4 star fruit, sliced

2 mangos

Place all ingredients into blender & blend until smooth. Makes 1 smoothie.

When The Beatles arrived in Hamburg, Germany, they played at numerous clubs in the Reeperbahn district, which is famous for its seedy entertainment and music clubs. Hamburg had once been Germany's main seaport and the third largest prosperous port in the world. However, the entire city had been reduced to rubble as a result of WWII bombing raids. By 1960, Hamburg had grown up from the ruins and established its reputation throughout Europe as a city of vice and criminal activity. A premier club, The Star-Club opened in 1962 and The Beatles were ecstatic to perform there. A tape recording was made of a late December, 1962, performance at The Star-Club in Hamburg and is available for purchase at most music outlets.

Several German travel sites quote John Lennon as saying: "I might have been born in Liverpool - but I grew up in Hamburg."

Get Back Joe Spiced Coffee
(Get Back — From the album Let It Be)

- 6 c. water
- ½ c. packed brown sugar
- ⅓ c. instant coffee
- 1 tbsp. ground cinnamon
- 2 tsp. cocoa
- ½ tsp. ground cloves
- ½ tsp. vanilla

In medium saucepan combine water, brown sugar, instant coffee, cinnamon, cocoa and cloves. Heat to boiling; reduce heat. Simmer uncovered 10 minutes. Remove from heat and stir in vanilla. Makes 6 servings.

GEORGE MARTINIS

3 oz. blackberry hint sparkling water

4 oz. good vodka

1 oz. Chambord

fresh blackberries for garnish

Mix all ingredients in shaker & pour into martini glass. Garnish with berries.

Thank you to Janet Harp-Jones for this cheeky drink recipe!

Sir George Martin is as much a legend as The Beatles. Martin, (record producer, composer, arranger) is often considered "the fifth Beatle," however, he considers the notion "nonsense." The accomplished Martin recognized the charisma in the lads (more so than their musical talent) and signed them to Parlophone record company in 1962. Martin's background and education in classical music contributed to the many innovative and diverse sounds recorded by The Beatles. The four considered George Martin to be a strong influence and mentor in their music production.

"Each song was a jewel on its own, and I used to bless them for that." - George Martin (from <u>John Lennon: The Life</u> by Philip Norman)

Drum Solos

MISCELLANEOUS

I Should Have Known Butter
(I Should Have Known Better — From the album A Hard Day's Night)

1½ c. (3 sticks) butter, softened

16 oz. fresh or frozen strawberries

½-¾ c. confectioner's sugar

Whip together all three ingredients. If it seems too runny you may add more confectioner's sugar.

Serve with fresh baked bread.

I Relish Her Majesty
(Her Majesty – From the album Abbey Road)

14 oz. jar cranberry-orange relish

½ c. pecans, chopped finely

8 oz. pkg. grapefruit or strawberry gelatin

½ c. boiling water

Combine relish with chopped pecans. Dissolve package of gelatin with boiling water. Stir into relish and chill until firm in a glass dish or gelatin mold.

Very Regal....

The 23-second song, "Her Majesty," is found at the end of the **Abbey Road** album. The 14-second tune is one of several mentions of royalty that The Beatles injected into their lyrics. Since the track appears after "The End," and was not listed on the original album sleeve, it is considered a "hidden track." "Her Majesty" has also been attributed as the first hidden track in recording history, proving that the band's talent for innovation never ceased. A hidden track (or "hidden treasure" which my daughter, Abby, has appropriately re-named it,) is occasionally found at the end of an artist's album (or CD) and is not listed on the album cover's song list. The hidden "treasure" is meant to surprise the listener and it endears you to the band.

Sometimes the hidden track is a mistake by the record company, but for the most part it is considered a treasure by music fans and should be ...***relished***...

Love, Love Me Two
(Love Me Do – From the album The Beatles)

1 c. mayonnaise

⅓ c. mango chutney

Combine ingredients and refrigerate until ready to serve. Great on sandwiches.

Don't you love a recipe with *two ingredients*?

The Beatles were originally formed with Pete Best as their drummer and he accompanied them during their wild years in Hamburg, Germany, while they were on the cusp of hitting the big time. Pete performed on the very first recording of "***Love Me Do***" in June, 1962, however, the song was later re-recorded and released without Pete. It was decided by the record company that Pete didn't fit the mold they were creating, so the colorful Ringo Starr was hired and history was made. Pete Best continues to tour with his band all over the world and has released terrific new music - check it out!

www.petebest.com

I Am The Eggs, Man!
(I Am the Walrus — From the album Magical Mystery Tour)

1½ lbs. Monterey Jack cheese, shredded (about 6 c.)

¾ lb. fresh mushrooms, sliced (about 2 c.)

½ large onion, chopped

4 tbsp. butter or margarine, melted

1 c. cubed ham

7 eggs, beaten

1¾ c. milk

½ c. flour

1 tbsp. parsley

1 tsp. seasoned salt

Preheat the oven to 350° F.

Place half the cheese in bottom of buttered 9" x 13" casserole dish. Sauté mushrooms and onion in butter or margarine until tender; place over cheese. Spread ham over mushrooms; top with rest of cheese. If desired, cover and refrigerate until ready to bake. Beat eggs, milk, flour, parsley, and seasoned salt; pour evenly over casserole. Bake for 45 minutes.

Everything I need to know I learned from these Beatle songs:

1. All You Need Is Love

2. Here Comes The Sun

3. Money — Can't Buy Me Love

4. Let It Be

5. Because

6. Don't Pass Me By

7. Got to Get You Into My Life

8. P.S. I Love You

9. Think for Yourself

10. We Can Work It Out

And if all else fails . . . Twist & Shout!

Here, There & Every Sausage Square
(Here, There & Everywhere – From the album Revolver)

- 8 oz. can refrigerated crescent roll dough
- 1 lb. pork sausage
- ¼ c. chopped onion
- 6 eggs, lightly beaten
- ¾ c. milk
- 2 tbsp. green pepper, chopped
- ½ tsp. dried oregano
- ½ tsp. pepper
- ¼ tsp. garlic salt
- 1 c. (4 oz) shredded mozzarella cheese

Preheat oven to 375°. Place crescent dough in a greased 9" x 13" baking dish, seal perforations. Bake in oven for 5-6 minutes, until golden brown.

In a skillet, brown sausage and onion until fully cooked. In a bowl, whisk together eggs, milk, green pepper, oregano, pepper and garlic salt. Pour mixture over crust.

Sprinkle sausage mixture on top of egg mixture and bake 15-20 minutes. Remove from oven and add mozzarella cheese, then bake 5 minutes longer or until cheese is melted. Cool slightly, then slice into squares and serve.

Paul McCartney penned the candy-coated ballad, *Here, There & Everywhere*, which was recorded in 1966 on the **Revolver** album. Paul, having long been considered the ballad-writer for The Beatles, decided the band needed a song that was raucous and cutting edge. *Helter Skelter*, was recorded in 1968 for the album **The Beatles** (known as the White Album,) and it definitely embodies his enthusiasm for recording what some critics consider the first heavy metal song ever. After 18 "takes" in the recording studio, Ringo flung his drum sticks across the studio and exclaimed "I've got blisters on my fingers".... which is heard on the recording.

HELTER SKELTER SKILLET

(Helter Skelter — from the album The Beatles [White Album])

2 lb. pkg. hashbrown potatoes

1 stick margarine

1 onion, chopped

1 green bell pepper, chopped

6 slices bacon, crisply cooked and crumbled

½ lb. breakfast sausage, cooked

2 c. shredded cheddar cheese

2 c. prepared white gravy

salt and pepper to taste

Melt margarine in skillet and add hash browns and onion. Sauté until cooked through; add green pepper. After green pepper is cooked through add bacon and sausage; heat thoroughly. Remove from stove and sprinkle cheese on top. Serve with side of gravy.

(Be careful removing skillet so you do not get blist-as on your fing-as.)

THE AFTER PARTY   **73**

Encores

DESSERTS

Savoy Truffles

The delicious song, "Savoy Truffle," is found on the album titled The Beatles, which is popularly known as The White Album. George Harrison wrote the song which was inspired by his friend, Eric Clapton, and Clapton's love of chocolates. At the time, Clapton was having dental issues and did not want to give up the rich confections. Check out the song and keep your ears tuned for the sexy saxophones!

My Savoy Truffle flavors were inspired by each individual personality of The Beatles. Fans tend to choose one Beatle as their "favorite" for one particular reason or another. Now you can enjoy a decadent truffle in dedication to your favorite Beatle!

The foursome were brilliant musicians and though they were accomplished individually, nothing can match the pure magic they created as the band The Beatles.

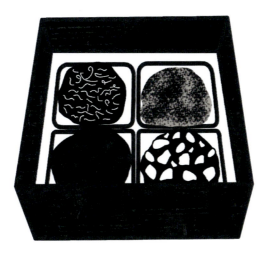

The John – A Lemon Tart
(In My Life – Annie's Favorite John Song)

1 c. milk chocolate chips

½ can sweetened condensed milk

1 tbsp. lemon extract

zest of lemon

(this makes about 20 truffles)

On low heat in a saucepan, melt chocolate until smooth, add sweetened condensed milk and stir until smooth & shiny. Remove from heat and stir in lemon extract. Chill mixture for 2 hours in refrigerator. Shape into 1" balls and roll into lemon zest. Chill for another hour and serve. Store in refrigerator. May be frozen.

The Paul — A Sweet Cherry Cream
(Eleanor Rigby — Abby's Favorite Paul Song)

1 c. milk chocolate chips

½ can sweetened condensed milk

1 tbsp. cherry extract

confectioners sugar

(this makes about 20 truffles)

On low heat in a saucepan, melt chocolate until smooth, add sweetened condensed milk and stir until smooth & shiny. Remove from heat and stir in cherry extract. Chill mixture for 2 hours in refrigerator. Shape into 1" balls. Sprinkle confectioners sugar on top. Chill for another hour and serve. Store in refrigerator. May be frozen.

The George – A Smooth, Mellow Coffee
(Something – Maggie's Favorite George Song)

1 c. milk chocolate chips

½ can sweetened condensed milk

1 tbsp. strong coffee (I suggest 2 tsp. instant coffee mixed with 1 tbsp. water)

cocoa powder

(this makes about 20 truffles)

On low heat in a saucepan, melt chocolate until smooth, add sweetened condensed milk and stir until smooth & shiny. Remove from heat and stir in coffee. Chill mixture for 2 hours in refrigerator. Shape into 1" balls. Sprinkle cocoa powder on top. Chill for another hour and serve. Store in refrigerator. May be frozen.

The Ringo – A Raspberry Nut
(With A Little Help From My Friends – Lanea's Favorite Ringo Song)

1 c. milk chocolate chips

½ can sweetened condensed milk

1 tbsp. raspberry extract

finely chopped pecans

(this makes about 20 truffles)

On low heat in a saucepan, melt chocolate until smooth, add sweetened condensed milk and stir until smooth & shiny. Remove from heat and stir in raspberry extract. Chill mixture for 2 hours in refrigerator. Shape into 1" balls and roll into chopped nuts. Chill for another hour and serve. Store in refrigerator. May be frozen.

Coffee Dessert Pie
Yes You Know It's Good News!
(Savoy Truffle — from the album The Beatles [The White Album])

graham cracker crust

1½ qt. coffee ice cream, softened

2 c. fudge ice cream topping

7 oz. jar marshmallow crème

2 c. miniature marshmallows

Fill graham cracker crust with 2 cups softened ice cream. Spoon ¾ cup fudge sauce over ice cream. Freeze until set, then repeat layering. Cover and freeze 8 hours or overnight. Refrigerate remaining fudge sauce.

The next day, preheat the oven broiler. Warm the remaining fudge sauce in the microwave or a small saucepan. Place the pie (in the pie pan) onto a cookie sheet. Spread the marshmallow creme over pie and sprinkle miniature marshmallows on top. Place under broiler until marshmallows are deep brown. Loosen pie with knife and remove from sides of pan. Serve immediately with warmed fudge sauce drizzled over top.

Apple Scruff Cake

1 c. oil

2 eggs, beaten

2 c. sugar

2 c. flour

2 tsp. cinnamon

1 tsp. nutmeg

1 tsp. baking soda

1 tsp. salt

5 c. sliced apples

1 c. chopped nuts

3 tbsp. lemon juice

Preheat oven to 350°. Blend oil with eggs; in separate bowl, mix sugar, flour, cinnamon, nutmeg, soda and salt. Combine with oil mixture. Stir in apples and nuts. Sprinkle lemon juice over top after placing in 13" x 9" x 2" pan. Batter will be very thick. Bake for 1 hour.

Thank you to my mother, Mert, who makes a lot of people happy with her culinary treats. She always sparks my creativity by having a recipe for every band that I like!

During the late 60's, The Beatles embarked upon a business venture which was named Apple Corps. The company was created for business and creative purposes, including a vision for seeking new talent which they could nurture and promote to success.

The Apple Corps. headquarters in London became a popular location for fans wishing to catch a glimpse of the famous quartet. A group of dedicated fans that faithfully congregated at the offices came to be known as the "Apple Scruffs." Check out George Harrison's song "Apple Scruffs" on his All Things Must Pass album.

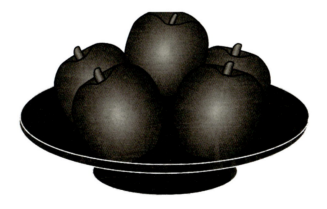

Strawberry Pie Forever!
(Strawberry Fields Forever – released as a single with Penny Lane in 1967)

1 c. sugar

few grains of salt

4 tbsp. cornstarch

1 c. water

red food coloring

2 c. fresh strawberries, (more if desired)

½ pint whipping cream

sugar to taste

baked pie crust (recipe on opposite page)
(may use ready-made crust)

Wash and drain the strawberries. Cut each strawberry in half and place them in a baked pie crust. Combine the cup of sugar, salt, and cornstarch. Mix well. Add water. Cook over direct heat, stirring constantly, until thickened. Add enough red food coloring to make a vibrant red. Cool. Pour COOLED filling on top of the strawberries.

Do not allow filling to get too cold and congealed. Refrigerate until firm.

Whip the whipping cream until it hold a peak. Add sugar to taste.

Top the pie with the whipping cream. Smooth cream all the way to the edge of pie.

This pie is good only for 2 days. Then the crust gets soggy. Eat it fast and enjoy!

In honor of my mom, Maxine Southerland, and in memory of John
~ Jude Southerland Kessler

Thanks to Jude Southerland Kessler's generosity for this scrumptious delight!

Louvenia Bobb's Homemade Pie Crust

1 c. flour

⅓ c. shortening, mounded up above top

½ tsp. salt (little less)

a cup with cold water and ice cubes floating in it

Mix the shortening and salt into the flour until crumbly. Then add 2 tbsps. and 1 tsp. of the ice water in your cup. Using clean hands, compress this into a ball of dough. Flour a cutting board or a sheet of waxed paper. Using a rolling pin that has been covered with flour, rolling out the dough just a bit larger than the size of your pie pan. Gently place the rolled-out dough into the pie pan. Crimp the sides using your thumb and first finger...making "waves."

Then using a fork, prick the dough in many places before you bake it. This will keep it from "puffing up" with air pockets as it bakes.

Bake pie crust at 350° for 5-7 minutes or until golden brown.

- Jude Southerland Kessler, Author

> Jude Southerland Kessler has been researching the life of John Lennon for 29 years, resulting in three publications in her John Lennon Series. John Lennon was not just a Rock & Roll star...he was a genius and visionary.
>
> Find Jude's material at:
>
> www.thejohnlennonseries.com

Why Don't We Brew It In The Road?
(Why Don't We Do It In The Road — from the album The Beatles [White Album])

17 oz. container Mascarpone cheese

2 c. confectioners' sugar

⅓ c. heavy cream

1 tsp. vanilla extract

11.75 oz. pkg. frozen marble poundcake, cut into 8 slices

2 tbsp. instant coffee granules (use instant espresso powder instead of granules for a stronger flavor)

½ c. hot water

½ tsp. unsweetened cocoa powder

raspberries, optional

At medium-high speed, beat Mascarpone cheese, confectioners' sugar, cream and vanilla until fluffy, 2-3 minutes; reserve. Place 4 slices poundcake in bottom of 8½" x 4½" loaf pan. In bowl, dissolve coffee in water.

Drizzle cake in pan with half of coffee mixture. Spread half of Mascarpone mixture over cake. Repeat layering with remaining cake, coffee and Mascarpone. Cover with plastic wrap; refrigerate at least 2 hours. Sprinkle with cocoa before serving. If desired, serve with raspberries.

You may use freshly brewed, strong coffee if preferred. Vary the flavor by using raspberry or hazelnut coffees.

Thank you Becky for this coffee delight.

I Want To Tell You About This Fab-4-U-Lous Flour-Less Chocolate Cake
(I Want To Tell You – from the album Revolver)

1 lb. Guittard semi-sweet chocolate, coarsely chopped

1 lb. (4 sticks) unsalted butter, diced

¼ tsp. sea salt

1 c. freshly-brewed espresso

¼ c. sugar in the raw

¾ c. light brown sugar

7 extra large eggs, beaten

hot water

garnishes: cocoa powder, raspberries, caramel ice cream topping, Savoy Truffles (opt.)

Preheat oven to 350°. Line bottom of a 9" diameter cake pan with 2" high sides with parchment. Place all chocolate in large bowl.

Bring butter, espresso and sugar to boil in medium saucepan, stirring to dissolve sugar.

Add chocolate; whisk until smooth and cool slightly.

Whip eggs till blended. Stir eggs into chocolate mixture until blended. (Do not whip).

Pour batter into prepared pan. Place cake pan in roasting pan. Pour enough hot water into roasting pan to come halfway up sides of cake pan.

Bake until center of cake is set and tester inserted into center comes out with a few moist crumbs attached, about 45 minutes.

Remove pan from water and chill cake overnight.

Cut around pan sides to loosen cake. Using oven mitts, hold pan bottom over low heat for 15 seconds, warming slightly to release cake. Place platter over pan. Hold pan and platter together tightly and invert. Lift off cake pan, peel off parchment and dust top of cake with cocoa powder. ... Then garnish and enjoy it with a lovely cup of tea while listening to your favorite Beatle Album!

Thank you to author, Judith Kristen, who shares her spectacular story about George Harrison in her book A Date With A Beatle, along with a lovable children's story Once Upon A Time In Liverpool.

Judith Kristen
www.JudithKristen.com
www.adatewithabeatle.com
www.onceuponatimeinliverpool.com

"Love and kindness is your job description – no matter what you do for a living. If you ever feel unsure of what you're supposed to do in a situation, here's a good rule of thumb: Always do what leads to greater love and compassion."

It's Your Birthday Cakes

(Birthday – from the album The Beatles [the White Album])

vanilla wafers

3 – 8 oz. pkgs. cream cheese, softened

1 c. sugar

3 eggs

1 tbsp. lemon juice

1 tsp. vanilla

paper cupcake liners

fruit pie filling

Preheat oven to 350°. In medium bowl, beat together cream cheese, sugar, eggs, lemon juice and vanilla. Place cupcake liners into a cupcake baking pan. Put 1 vanilla wafer in each liner. Fill ⅔ full with mixture. Bake for 15 minutes. Cool completely. Top with your favorite fruit pie filling.

Re-Act Naturally

(Act Naturally — from the album Help!)

- 4 firm, ripe bananas, sliced in half lengthwise
- 4 tbsp. unsalted butter
- ½ c. dark brown sugar
- 1 tsp. ground cinnamon
- ½ tsp. ground nutmeg
- 3 tbsp. lemon juice (juice of about 1 fresh lemon)
- ½ c. banana liqueur
- ½ c. dark rum

Melt butter in a heavy skillet; add the brown sugar, cinnamon and nutmeg, stir until sugar is completely melted. Add the bananas and cook until hot, coat well with syrup, but careful not to squish the bananas. Carefully pour in banana liqueur and rum. If the butter is very hot, the bananas will flame. You may cook over medium heat, stirring until the alcohol cooks out. Another option is to light the liqueur and rum with a long match and cook until the flame dies out and alcohol is cooked out. Enjoy the chemical *re-actions*.

The White Album Fondue
(The album The Beatles is commonly referred to as "The White Album")

10 oz. white chocolate, chopped (with nuts, optional)

¼ c. Half & Half

assorted fresh fruit, cookies, pound cake cubes

Combine chocolate and Half & Half in small fondue pot or saucepan. Cook over low heat, stirring frequently until chocolate is melted. Dip fruit, cookies or cake into mixture and eat 'em up.

The album known as the "White Album," was officially named "The Beatles" and it appears on lists all over the world as one of the greatest albums of all time. Released in November, 1968, the album was very eclectic and innovative, resulting in worldwide critical acclaim, positive and some negative.

It should be enjoyed with a delightful white chocolate fondue......

For The Benefit Of Mr. Kite
There Will Be Dessert Tonite With Circus Animals
(Being For the Benefit of Mr. Kite — Sgt. Pepper's Lonely Hearts Club Band)

18.9 oz. box funfetti cake mix

2 c. fat free plain yogurt

1 c. light whipped topping

animal crackers

Mix together all ingredients and chill in refrigerator for at least 4 hours. Serve with animal crackers for dipping.

It looks & tastes like cotton candy ... just like being at the circus.

Thanks to my rockin' niece, Molly, for this recipe which is sure to be a spectacle!

John Lennon's lyrics for "Being for the Benefit of Mr. Kite" were inspired by an old circus show poster that he found in an antique shoppe. The song amuses us with introductions and descriptions of the prime characters in the much anticipated show.

In the same way that we enjoy the dazzling story of Mr. Kite and Circus, The Beatles story is thrillingly portrayed in a grandiose show only to be seen at The Mirage in Las Vegas, Nevada. Cirque du Soleil, an artistic circus, portrays the history of The Beatles, professionally integrated with the exquisite sounds of the Fab 4 in its LOVE show. The theatre at The Mirage Hotel, was built specifically for the show and is undoubtedly one of the best productions to ever pay tribute to The Beatles. Include this show on your bucket list!

http://www.cirquedusoleil.com/en/shows/love

Phase One In Which Doris Gets Her Oat Cookies
(Two Of Us – from the album Let It Be)

- 2½ c. flour
- 1 c. oats (instant)
- 1 tsp. baking soda
- 1 tsp. cinnamon
- ½ tsp. salt
- 1 c. sugar
- 1 egg
- 1 tsp. vanilla
- 1 c. persimmon pulp
- 1 c. raisins
- 1 c. margarine, softened
- 1 c. brown sugar

Mix together all ingredients and drop by heaping teaspoonfuls onto a greased cookie sheet. Bake at 350° degrees for 20 mins.

Thank you to the most awesome A.J. Reynolds for this Indiana delicacy!

NOTE: Persimmon Pulp - Halve persimmons lengthwise and scoop out the flesh with a spoon. Discard the skin, and any hard brown seeds you might find. Puree pulp. Just about anything will do: a food processor, a blender, a food mill, in a pinch even a fork will all get the job done.

You will use approximately 2-3 persimmons to accumulate 1 cup of pulp.

At the beginning of the "Two of Us" recording (from the album Let It Be,) you'll hear a witty John Lennon say "Phase one in which Doris gets her oats." Much speculation has been placed upon what John was chattering about, however, Lennon had a comedic way of spouting fortuitous expressions at any given time. It was part of his ingenious manner and he was likely throwing in a funny at the beginning of the song. As with all songs, "Two of Us" has been dissected by music lovers and surmised that McCartney wrote the song about Linda or about John. Either way, it's an enchanting song that is rarely heard by the casual fan. Check it out today!

Tickets To Ride
(Ticket to Ride – from the album Help!)

- 1 c. all-purpose flour
- ½ tsp. baking soda
- ¼ tsp. baking powder
- ¼ tsp. salt
- ½ c. butter or margarine, softened
- ½ c. granulated sugar
- ½ c. firmly packed brown sugar
- 1 large egg
- ½ tsp. vanilla extract
- 1 c. crisped rice cereal
- 1 c. quick-cooking oats

Preheat oven to 350°. Combine flour, baking soda, baking powder and salt in a bowl and set aside. Beat the butter on medium speed until light and fluffy. Add sugars and beat until blended. Add egg and vanilla, mixing well. Stir in flour mixture, then cereal and oats. Drop the mixture by tablespoonfuls onto lightly sprayed cookie sheet. Bake for 12 minutes or until cookies are lightly browned. Cool completely and store in airtight container.

Thank you to my friend, Janie, for this great cookie recipe!

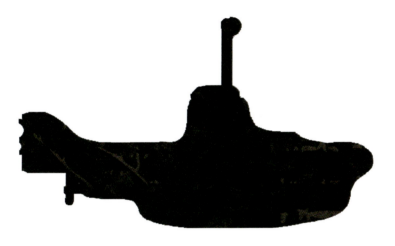

Movies

Refreshments

Well.....I'll Hope You'll Come & See Me In The Movies.....

Riding high on their musical career and in response to demanding fans who begged for any and all glimpses of the stars, it was inevitable that The Beatles were cast in their own movies. The band starred in five motion pictures: *A Hard Day's Night*, *Help!*, *Magical Mystery Tour*, *Yellow Submarine* and *Let It Be*. Each movie was stylishly unique and combined each Beatle's sense of humor with smooth acting skill. Furthermore, the band wrote and recorded an album to accompany each film, thereby cementing success not only in the movie theatre, but the record store, too. At this time, a couple of the movies are difficult to find, but I suggest that you inquire with friends, libraries and merchandise websites to find these treasures.

So, roll up on the sofa with your sweetie, enjoy some refreshments and treat yourself to movie night with the lads. Study this era which has long passed us by and been replaced by youtube videos and instant messaging. Don't forget to savor the quirky British humor, handsome faces and timeless music!

Penny Lane Popcorn Balls

3 large bags of microwave popcorn

1 stick butter

1 large bag of large marshmallows

1 tsp. vanilla

food coloring (opt.)

2 c. M&M's®

Pop popcorn and take out any unpopped kernels. Put in large enough pan to hold it all. Melt in large pan 1 stick butter, low heat. Add marshmallows and melt. Turn heat off and add vanilla and food coloring. Pour mixture over popcorn and stir until popcorn is covered. Let cool 5 minutes. Add M&M's® and stir well. With buttered hands form into balls.

Kudos to Julie for these delicious movie treats!

Root Beer Submarine Floats

frosty mug

chilled root beer

vanilla ice cream

Place a couple of scoops of ice cream into a frosty mug and pour chilled root beer over the cream.

A Hard Day's Night

This black & white film was released in 1964 and was an instant success, as expected. The world was able to witness John, Paul, George and Ringo on the big screen having more fun than say, a barrel of *Monkees* .... The dead pan humor and Marx Brothers-like delivery gave them critical acclaim, but more importantly, fans could drool over the close-up shots of those dreamy Brits. Even today's younger generation can get a chuckle out of the Fab 4's slapstick humor.

Help!

The 1965 film, shot in color, was the second motion picture starring The Beatles. The script contained more intricate plot than their first movie. The comedic story developed into a James Bond-type action-adventure which had the Beatles running from characters in an evil cult. The production was highly successful for the group, grossing over 12 million dollars.

Magical Mystery Tour

Released in the UK in 1967, Magical Mystery Tour was more of an "artsy" type of movie that was focused around a group of unsuspecting travelers on a British mystery tour. The 53-minute film has received both positive and negative reviews, however, viewing the flick today is refreshing and entertaining. Of course, the music written for the movie was outstanding, "I Am The Walrus" performed by the band in animal masks is not to be missed!

Yellow Submarine

Released in 1968, the film was an animated musical fantasy, based upon The Beatles music, specifically, the Lennon-McCartney song Yellow Submarine. The Beatles' personas were given to the animated characters..the Beatles actually providing little voice input; the presence of their songs is included in the movie and soundtrack.

LET IT BE

A documentary was recorded of The Beatles rehearsing and recording songs for the album **Let It Be**. The music from the documentary was nominated and won the Academy Award for Best Original Song Score. It is our last look at The Beatles collaborating together and it's very poignant. It contains the famous unannounced rooftop concert as well.

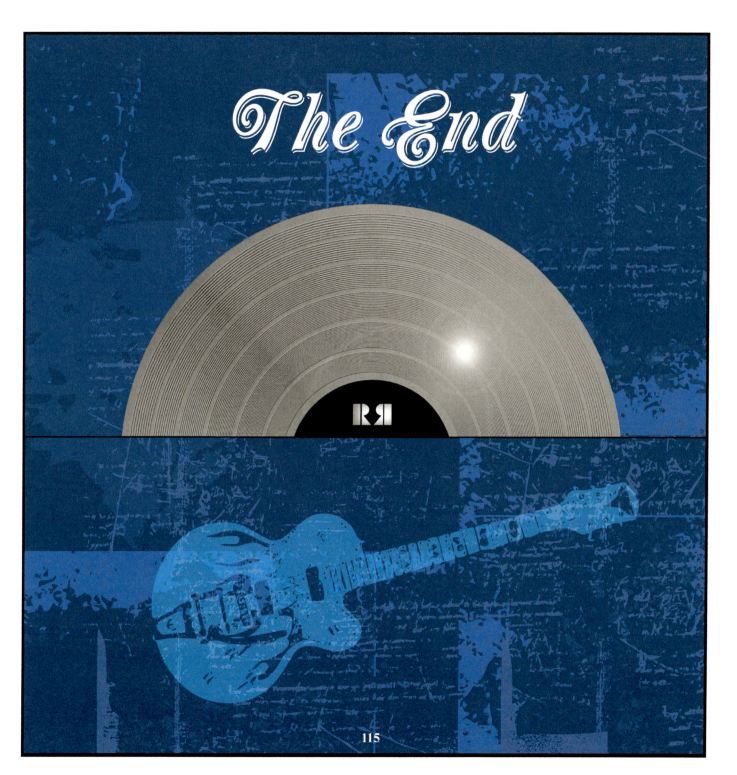

And In The End...

The song "The End" was the last official track on the album "Abbey Road," which was the last album the lads recorded together (see note about "Her Majesty" on page 63.) It was very prophetic for what was happening to the band at that time. The poetry was written by Paul McCartney, and has long been considered a genuine piece of art and philosophy; the lyrics have been repeated on everything from t-shirts to brick sidewalks.

"The End" led to the beginning of solo careers for the lads from Liverpool. The band acknowledged their parting of ways during the spring of 1970 due to creative differences and each were eager to seek fresh change in their music careers and personal lives.

Enjoy four recipes created to pay tribute to these unforgettable musicians, who collectively composed and built a forum for rock and roll....each of them loved rock and roll as much as life.

THE END

Cold Turkey Salad
(Cold Turkey by John Lennon)

2 c. smoked turkey, shredded

½ c. light mayonnaise (may add more if preferred)

½ tsp. liquid smoke

½ c. dried cranberries

¼ c. celery, finely chopped

½ c. glazed walnuts, chopped

Mix all ingredients and serve on a bed of peaceful lettuce...

Following the break-up of The Beatles, John Lennon spent the next decade composing music and creating art in numerous forms, but also taking much needed respites from his work. He was a tremendous wit and contributed humor in many areas of his life. Lennon focused an abundance of his time and energy to advocating peace and ironically, this proponent of accord was murdered outside his New York City home on December 8, 1980, at the age of 40. His words and poetry are uniquely profound, having come from a deeply sensitive man who wished for world peace...

John Lennon Song List:

Imagine

Cold Turkey

Just Like Starting Over

Woman

Instant Karma

Watching the Wheels

Whatever Gets You Through the Night

Beautiful Boy (Darling Boy)

#9 Dream

Paul McCartney (Macca) had an extensive technical musical background and used his talents at a very rapid pace after the close of The Beatles. Macca continues to be highly active in the music business, having performed successful concerts quite recently. He & his wife, Linda, worked together in their band Wings from about 1971 until 1981. Paul found the name for the band after experiencing a close call during the birth of their daughter, Stella, where both mother & child were in danger of dying. Paul says he began praying intensely and the image of wings from a guardian angel came to him. He used that image to name the band, which celebrated many hits over the decade.

Paul McCartney Song List:

Maybe I'm Amazed

My Love

Band On The Run

Jet

Nineteen Hundred and Eighty-Five

Listen To What The Man Said

Silly Love Songs

Calico Skies

I'm Gonna Sit Right Down & Write Myself A Letter

Vegan Wings

(Paul is a dedicated vegan and I bet he'd dig these wings)

3 c. (2 – 15 oz. cans) garbanzo beans or chickpeas

½ c. oats (process half in small grinder)

¾ c. vital wheat gluten (Bob's Red Mill Gluten Flour® recommended)

½ c. whole grain unseasoned bread crumbs

½-¾ c. buffalo sauce (the more sauce, the better!)

2 cloves garlic

½ c. onion, chopped

Drain and rinse the beans, mash in a mixing bowl. You may leave a few half beans for texture but no whole beans. Add all other ingredients and mix with fork and then knead with hands until firm and uniform. You may need to add more vital wheat gluten or breadcrumbs. Refrigerate for 30 minutes.

Divide into patties or smaller "wings." Bake at 375° on a Silpat (or baking sheet sprayed well with oil) until firm and heated through, about 45 minutes. Turn once during baking.

Thanks to April Hargraves from the Frugally Green Mom Blog for this great contribution! Check out her green recipes at:

www.frugallygreenmom.com

THE END

My Sweet Pakoras (aka Pakodas)
(My Sweet Lord - by George Harrison)

1 large onion

1 c. chickpea flour

2 tbsp. rice flour (both flours found at Indian market) rice flour adds crispness

salt to taste

cumin powder to taste

finely chopped coriander, to taste

cashews, sliced

oil for frying

Cut the onion finely and add salt. Add chickpea and rice flours, cumin powder and more salt if desired. Add coriander and cashews. Mix this very well and add very little water to the batter to bind it together. Heat oil in medium frying pan. Take a small portion of this batter, form into one-inch sized balls and drop into hot oil; may fry four to five at a time.

Fry until golden brown on medium heat. Serve hot with tomato sauce or green chutney.

George Harrison Song List:

My Sweet Lord

What Is Life

Give Me Love (Give Me Peace On Earth)

Got My Mind Set On You

Wah-Wah

Isn't It A Pity

Apple Scruffs

Crackerbox Palace

All Things Must Pass

George Harrison embraced the Eastern culture after meeting the Maharishi Mahesh Yogi and also becoming friends with Ravi Shankar, who gifted George with the introduction of Eastern music. Shortly after the demise of The Beatles, George was approached by Ravi Shankar who asked if George could help his country, Bangladesh, which was suffering from famine. Harrison, being the generous friend he was, called upon his many musician mates and organized the first mega-star benefit show, which was held at Madison Square Garden. The Concert for Bangladesh is a star studded show that you definitely should not miss!

After reading about George's love of Indian food, I tried to find a recipe and called upon our friends, Santosh and Varsha Pundukare. After hearing my plea for help, this gracious and lovely couple (& beautiful daughters Mansi & Saanvi) invited us immediately to their home and served dish after dish of their outstanding cultural specialties. We genuinely felt the peace and generosity that George must have felt from his Eastern friends and celebrated in that harmony. Thank you Varsha & Santosh for this delicious recipe!

The affable Ringo Starr brought great compassion and style to the Beatles and is sometimes overlooked for his tremendous drumming skill and technique. Ringo went on to create terrific solo music and appear in many acting projects. Around 1990, Ringo put together a group which he named: Ringo and His All Starr Band. The group is interchangeable and tours every other year with different popular musicians who perform memorable music and shows for his many fans. Ringo says that he always loved being in a band, and boy do we love that he's still rockin' it!

Ringo Starr Song List:

It Don't Come Easy

Photograph

You're Sixteen You're Beautiful
(And You're Mine)

The No-No Song

Oh My My

Back Off Boogaloo

Have You Seen My Baby

Slow Down

Some People

It Don't Come Cheezy Potatoes
(It Don't Come Easy - by Ringo Starr)

2 lb. pkg. frozen hash brown potatoes

½ c. melted margarine

16 oz. sour cream

1 can cream of mushroom soup

1 tsp. salt

½ tsp. pepper

16 oz. cheddar cheese, shredded

Topping:

¾ c. corn flakes, crushed

¼ c. melted margarine

Preheat oven to 350°. Spray 9" x 13" baking dish with non-stick spray. In bowl, mix hashbrowns and next 6 ingredients. Pour ingredients into baking dish. Sprinkle crushed corn flakes over top of mixture and pour melted butter over top of flakes. Bake for 1 hour.

WANT TO PURCHASE MORE?

Go to: www.reciperecordscookbook.com

Books are $18.00 plus shipping/handling

Contact the Author, Lanea Stagg

reciperecordsml@aol.com

Recipe Records

3 Marlaneas Studio

2920 Harmony Way

Evansville, IN 47720

Don't Miss These Recipe Records Publications:

Recipe Records – $19.95

Recipe Records, the 60's Edition – $25.00

Purchase at:

www.reciperecordscookbook.com

Made in the USA
Las Vegas, NV
17 December 2024